The Quenching

poems by

Bonnie Wai-Lee Kwong

Finishing Line Press
Georgetown, Kentucky

The Quenching

Acknowledgments

Grateful acknowledgment is made to the following publications, where some of the poems originally appeared: *The California Quarterly, The Pedestal, Soñadores: We Came to Dream, sPARKLE & bLINK,* and *Spillway.*

"The Cipher of Fireflies," "Spilled Rust," and "Semaphores" were part of a prepared piano performance with Tessa Brinckman at The Center for New Music in San Francisco.

"The Quenching" and "tiens, tiān 天! look, the sky!" were performed at the Art in Nature Festival with Judy Shintani and Marybeth Tereszkiewicz respectively.

Many thanks to Eavan Boland, former Director of the Creative Writing Program, and Jennifer Dionne, Associate Professor of Materials Science and Engineering for my artist's residency at Stanford University.

Publisher: Leah Huete de Maines
Editor: Christen Kincaid
Cover Art: Na Omi Judy Shintani and Susan Friedman
Nature Photography by Susan Friedman
Boy photos provided by Bonnie Wai-Lee Kwong and Na Omi Judy Shintani
Author Photo: Bob Hsiang Photography
Cover Design: Elizabeth Maines McCleavy

Order online: www.finishinglinepress.com
also available on amazon.com

Author inquiries and mail orders:
Finishing Line Press
P. O. Box 1626
Georgetown, Kentucky 40324
U. S. A.

Table of Contents

For my father

Introduction

Translational motion involves a body moving from one point in space to another. To carry across is to translate. Moving again—motion and inertia—formed my first dateable memory. I said to my parents: "But we just moved here." I was born in Madison, Wisconsin, while my father was a graduate student. We moved to Lafayette, Indiana so he could finish his dissertation after his advisor took a job there. We had barely been in Lafayette for a year—I was just beginning to feel at home—when my parents told me we would be moving again. My father was to start his post doc in Connecticut. I was three years old by then, and bilingual: I spoke Cantonese to my parents, and mostly English to others. Speech was an act of translation from a space beyond language into language. There was no need then to translate across languages.

In Connecticut, my mother bundled me up one day and took me for a walk in the snow. She told me by the following winter, we would be living in a place without snow. The place without snow turned out to be where my parents were from, Hong Kong. There I began to speak more Cantonese while still retaining and learning English. Speech and translational movement. Around age four, I became aware every time the adults in the family went out, they had to carry, in addition to keys and cash, an ID card; it was illegal to walk on the streets without one.

Not everyone could move across borders with ease. Stories of undocumented migrants from mainland China hiding in boxcars and swimming to Hong Kong recalled my mother's escape from Mao's Communism as a child decades ago, taking a boat from her hometown in Chaozhou to Hong Kong, with gold hidden in the lining of her padded jacket.

At translational borders, there are pauses where one can question points of origin. When I first heard my teacher used the word "sofa" instead of "couch" in first grade English class in Hong Kong, I wondered if she had taken the Cantonese word 梳化 *so¹ faa³* and translated it into English. I quickly realized it was the opposite—the English word had likely entered Cantonese. Even then I knew movement across linguistic borders was asymmetric, and flowed freely in one direction only. Navigating the borders between Cantonese and English, between English from two parts of the world, was to become part of my daily life.

My mother spoke Teochew (or Chaozhou) with her family. I learned Mandarin from a private tutor, and continued to speak Cantonese to my family and friends. The cadence of spoken English stayed with me, though my use of the language was mostly in reading and writing. When my father's sabbatical took us to Columbia, Missouri for six months, "sofa" became "couch" again.

I spent my last year of high school at a boarding school in Connecticut, studying French while I was there. French words could readily be found in English, and I wanted to learn how to pronounce them. The gradient of imperialism can be found across the history of language propagation. English and Chinese words are commonly found in Japanese, not vice versa. My father speaks of a time when one had to use English to order phone service in Hong Kong. Most Chinese residents of Hong Kong spoke some English, and most educated residents of any ethnicity were fluent in English. My twelve years growing up in Hong Kong, the only two Cantonese phrases I heard a Westerner speak were: 有落 *jau⁵ lok⁶* (getting off here) and 唔該 *m⁴ goi¹* (please). As I visit checkpoints across linguistic borders, I hope to find holes in the fences, inclines against the dominant gradient, traffic running in opposite directions.

During my college years in Ann Arbor, I became close friends with my Japanese conversation partner Tomoko Ogawa, an artist who told me the folktale of Momotaro 桃太郎, the boy hero born of a peach, who grew up to fight 鬼 *oni*, demons. I wondered who the demons were, unnamed, undescribed. In the shadow of Vincent Chin's murder in Detroit a decade earlier, I could've mapped the symbol of 鬼 *oni* to Vincent's white killers—I did not. Behind the idea of 鬼 *oni* rested emptiness, a question. I only saw upon writing about Vincent's murder decades later, 鬼 *oni* was the anger rising from the emptiness of Detroit—the loss of jobs, status, and working class dignity transforming into a monster, seeking enemies of another race. I would frame the resistance of Momotaro 桃太郎 against this 鬼 *oni* not as a battle of physical violence, but as the telling of stories to fill the void, the singing of songs, the meeting of friends, as Momotaro 桃太郎 gathered strength in the company of his animal friends, sharing millet dumplings.

Upon graduation, I moved to New York, a city of many languages, and helped my mother land with her green card. In New York, I met a man I was to marry. During trips to visit his family in Western Pennsylvania, English was the only language we spoke.

My father came to the United States to study sensory perception—how sensations such as light, heat, and sound are received and interpreted by insects and humans. His transitioned to speech recognition research, then to Buddhist philosophy. I have inherited from him an interest in ciphers and deciphering. My use of various languages and phrases of song comes from my mother's speech in daily life. From here, I offer a trajectory into a future through the sharing of ideas, through the senses, the body, and the mind.

tiens, tiān 天! look, the sky!

I spent too much time
thinking
about   the sky

I began to forget
how

to
walk

I began to forget
how
to crawl

what do I know
of
gravity

I only say:
sky
come down to me

watch me
walk again

sway my arms
with my feet

hear me sing
again....
sky
come
down to me
I am returning
to my feet

I've lived
where the sky
was narrow
where clouds hung low

          sensed imminent storms
    like
              drunken breath

   tasted the fog
with my tongue   in spring

       I fixed my gaze
          on the sky so long
      I forgot the animal
              in me

   the stars in the night sky
  formed a map
      I couldn't read

there were too many stories
       too many castles

    I cleared the sky again:
  tiens, tiān 天!
   look, the sky!

  tiān kōng 天空
      the empty
sky

      I can move again
     I remember
       my limbs

   more than a tree
  I am animate
      arms and legs swaying

wind flowing through me
    sweeping high and low

clouds
distant as a fourth language:
ciel, nauges

clouds
like the swipe
of a paintbrush

sky
come down to me

tiens, tiān 天!
look, the sky!

if you wish
to make love
to me
I must tell you this:

I was born
a nomad
the sky
my only constant

by the age
of four
I had moved
four
times

my first memory
is of moving
again

the sky
my only constant

there were times
the sky seemed
too large

and I too small
like a meteor
liú xīng 流星
a flowing star

when I close my eyes at night
I am nowhere

in the cradle of the ocean
I fall
through the bottom

in the cradle of the sky
with flight
the fear
of falling
yet the moon stays

I am so far away

what do I know
of gravity?

exile 流亡 liú wáng
a flowing death
sky
come down
to me

home
is where
you see me

if you wish
to make love to me

think of me

as the moon:

halfway
between
sky
and earth
sky
I speak to you
as I would   a lover
I dare not name

tiān kōng 天空
the empty sky

come closer
I'll sing you
a song

locus

Ann Arbor, Michigan

there were   times   my young
mind
traveled
not with my body

but

with   the
odyssey:
adamant   red ivy
scaling   the walls
of the
law   quad

could
have   been
the   paw prints
of
monsters
I
could have
escaped
into
the certainty
of monsters
in fixed geographies—

scylla

and charybdis
the cyclops
and   polyphemus—

if my body
had   not   conjured
penelope

                                                leaving
                            a tuft   of sea
                              anemone
                    at a shipwreck
before swimming off
              on   her
                                journey

                                              I
                                could   have
                    traveled
                                      in
                        perpetual motion
                  if   not
        for   friction however slight

                        with passing bodies

                                        a small child
                  outside   the financial   aid
                                  office   alone   no more
                                                                than four
                                crouched
                  next   to
        a bike   too   large
          to be his:
                                        do you know   how to unlock
                                            this?

                                    there   were more   unusual

                          locomotives—
        to travel   by peach
        downstream

like 桃太郎

momotaro

born
from a giant fruit   an
                              elderly couple
                            raised him

              he grew up
      to fight 鬼 *oni*   demons
          left
      to the listener's   imagination   *oni*
                                    can take the shape
                                  of emptiness:

              highrises
      hollowed   as if by jaws   others
                                        who

wore

                                         my hair and complexion
              grew up in Michigan
          driving cars   wide as boats—
          horizontal   unmistakably
                              American

              they knew   the materials science
                              of an auto town:

                                    forty miles

away

                              the torque
                                of a baseball bat
                                swung in rage

          the compressive
        strength of the skull
              chink, jap, nip....
        it's because of you little motherfuckers
            that we're out of work

                              I once journeyed
      back from new york   by rail—
                  long waits   on frozen platforms

            for freight trains   to pass
        under a steel sky   not a conductor
                        or passenger
                              in sight

                401 depot st
                ann arbor   *the finest station…*
                        between buffalo and

chicago

            the railroad sold it
        a restaurateur
            built   *The Gandy Dancer*
                                    in its place

            workers
        who threw their weight
            on metal spikes   to straighten
                        the tracks
        would not have
                clinked
                    glasses of chianti
        and set them on white
        tablecloth—
                                nostalgia
                        come too early

I hid
in a warm, moist greenhouse
to tend my charges:

coleus leaves
lithops
staring   bonsai
writing itself

lettuce
tender to the touch—

to unfurl
break
out of the loam
if only
the glass roof
could stay

The Cipher of Fireflies

Timlin, PA

I towered over Punxsutawney Phil.
The lore of the town
held the groundhog's sighting
of his own shadow
signaled a late spring.
I had no way of telling what Phil saw.

I had married Bits' son—
Bits, for Mommy's itsy bitsy baby.
He played with metal puzzles
like twisted nails or paperclips askew.
How to wedge them together? How to sunder?

The cold of this terrain could freeze
the arm of a semaphore.
Bits studied math, moved away
to a job shifting bytes.
His brother Rick stayed to work in the mines,
and on highways.
Railroad tracks grew silent with age.
I was married to a man who knew to kiss me
if I tilted my head at the slightest angle.
The cipher of fireflies starred the sky.

Rick's son, the youngest, moved away
to mine bits and bytes. His daughters stayed
to tend the coursing of blood in strangers,
from the heart to the remote ganglia, and back again.

Spilled Rust

Timblin, PA

Hours of starting and stopping. Inertia jolts.
An old highway, built, torn and rebuilt,
tapers into rural roads.
A pit overgrown with weeds
like stray hair on a bald head.
A rusted harness for a single horse.
Coal pickings close to the surface.
My then husband's family
once ran this small mine.
When coal left the soil, water carried silt
into the pipes and taps of their homes.
Here, I speak one language only—
not Cantonese, not Mandarin, not Japanese….
I ask my husband how to soak
the sudden emptying of my womb—spilled rust.
A confederate flag hangs
on the porch of an abandoned bank.
No pharmacy in sight.
His aunt offers pads from her home. I thank her.
In my aching body, what empties might fill again.
I will return with the youngest in their family.
I can only wish for new roots
to bind the spent soil.

the drift of magnolias

washington d.c.

the
extravagance
of trees   with bare
branches
sending forth

petals
before leaves

in the shortest
days   of spring

magnolias

the shape of
cupped
hands
stately   with tough   skin
as   to resist   the palps
museums
on a   capital
avenue   of
beetles

I was
with child
traveling

the   center
of   my body
slowly unsettling
nausea   as if
at sea

or
from seeing too much
too fast

a few days
after conception

                    we
            were in Cobá   my husband
                              and I

            where pyramids
                    hid
                              unexcavated
                        in tree-spotted
            mounds

        limestone
            glistened   like monuments
                                          in the capital
                                    of my birth country
                              Jefferson
                                          Lincoln

        on evening
                    television
                the first
                US
                fighter jets   peeled off
                                    for the   night
                                          skies
                                    of Baghdad

                              how
                        in   the distant
                                          future
                                    would
                          visitors from another galaxy
        nausea   excavate
                from   moving   monuments
                        too
                        fast
                              white
                        as limestone

                    Jefferson
          Lincoln

                              in the
                          ruined
                              capital
  of
                                      my birth
                          country
  in tree-spotted
  mounds like
          the pyramids of Cobá

          stateside
  my hostess in D.C.
                          my husband's
                              great-aunt

          (half, really)
                  knowing
              I am
              with   child
          serves prime rib
              pink   tender to the touch

                              we speak
              of   the piano   the
                                      harpsichord
                          of perfect
                              pitch   and memory

                    her husband
            speaks
    of his work
            in economics   a wartime
                        paper
        to
            poison   nausea
            civilian
    water supply   from
                in
            Vietnam   moving too
                                            fast
            as if
    at
            sea   or
                                in
                    the   house

                        of a would-
            be   war
            criminal

magnolias

                            grow   on
                                the   hillsides
                            of
                            Hong Kong

            these
    hardy blossoms   survived
                    the ice age
                                            and
                            rose
                        with   forming
                            mountains

migrated
with
continental drift

玉蘭
juk⁶ laan⁴

jade
orchid
in Cần Thơ   I crossed
the Mekong
the mother
of water   a river
open as the sea

I can   hear

its rush
still

poison
is a word
I do   not
wish
to learn

in
Vietnamese

mẹ   mother
nausea
of a mother
with child

as if

at sea

mộc lan

                                        magnolias

                      leaves
         like horse ears

         somewhere in Georgia
     or
    Hà Nội
             the back
               of a finger
                 might
        sense a
     magnolia petal
  as
       the contours
     of a lover's cheek
                   the luxury
                      of
            slow   touch

      migration

      unhurried
         as magnolias
               drifting
  with   the
              stillness
              of continents

undula

a woman

        labors

               in a deep
             tub

         いるか　いるか？
     iruka　iru ka?

                  are
                    there
             dolphins?

        fragments
         of song

               over
           iambs
                  of the womb
           a cellist
               plucks
         a string—
    others sound
          in
         sympathy

the endpin
        of
     a cello
        sends

   song
    from
            wooden
             belly to floor
the floor sings
           I slide sideways:
             hand
           arm   waist
                 along
              the floor

                    the floor replies:
          inaudible
                    whispers
                                             if I fell
          this floor   from a certain
                                             height
          would
          not embrace
                    me

                              the felt damper
                    on piano strings
               rids song   of resonance
                                   unintended

               to sharp
          a fourth
                    or flat
               a
                         fifth
          is
     to clash
          colors: the purple
                              flare   against
                    of
                         an orchid   verdant
                                                       leaves
          the mottled
          skin
                         of a newborn
                              before
               the
                         first breath

                              two lovers
                    on a piano bench
          play in unison
          one hand each
          one octave apart

two lovers
on a piano
bench
play in counterpoint

one hand each
rise   wait and fall
        rise
                and wait

a lover's back arches to
my swift
                                touch
    diabolus
            in musica

there is no telling when

in drifting
                two waves
        may
                            meet
                again

Semaphores

Rumplestiltskin failed to swindle the king of his firstborn
with his magical spinning of straw into gold, his secret technology.
The miller's daughter guessed his name.

I was not—am not—afraid of signals unfamiliar.
Of revolution:
One if by land, two if by sea.

Of empire:
Paris est tranquille et les bon citoyens sont content.
Paris is quiet and the good citizens are content.

Of distress:
· · · − − − · · ·
three-dits, three-dahs, three-dits.

Of the railroad underground, away from hounds:
Wade in the water, wade in the water, children.

Light angles between curtains
in the small hours of the gloaming.
My son's rooting for a nipple with an open mouth
is both action and signal.

Many miles ago, I watched my father speak into a microphone.
He turned words into graphs—music to deaf ears.
He knew formulas for the conjugation of air.
I knew his nickname.

If satellites fail, homing pigeons might map their return
by sounds too low for the human ear,
the sound of the ocean pulsing against land
scattering over the terrain.

Change unfetters the wings of carrier pigeons—
to compute with the speed of light
patterns once punched on cards, braille-like,
to be read by mechanical looms.

Paralyzed bodies can breathe messages in Morse.
I learn to listen.

all the same leaf

if the stem

                of a

calla

      lily

                           unfurls

                casually

                  into leaf

                   green

                     into verdant

              green

and

          splays

into petal

      where

        green

           pales

        to white

all

the same
leaf

                           if

                              an arm

                                 can reach

                  like

a fin   or

          a wing

                    if
              young   if I place
                    mammals   my hand
         sometimes   on a waist naked
   wear   curved
         gills   like my own

                              if I allow her
                       to wear
                              my dress
                                              and
                  undress
                                   her   myself

                       do I need
                                        to take
                  another name

The Quenching

In the grace of these branches bowing in the wind,
in the calm of these redwoods,
there is thirst like a dry creek bed.

There is a thirst for each animal;
there is a thirst for each plant;
there is the shared thirst of a dry creek bed;
the thirst of a fox leaving his scent along the path;
the thirst of rabbits fleeing the fox;
the thirst of unhatched eggs;
the thirst of newts waiting to mate;
the thirst of moss clinging to trees by slender filaments;
the thirst of redwood saplings tethered to posts;
the thirst of manzanitas offering their drop-like berries;
the thirst of madrones, shedding their red, red bark.

On the shared thirst of this dry creek bed,
lay down a river of cloth.
There will always be absence like thirst.
Drink from this river of cloth.
Drink with cupped hands.
Drink from the sky above.
Drink, and let the sky be.

In the grace of these branches bowing in the wind,
in the calm of these redwoods, there is hunger like love.

There is hunger stalking like a coyote;
the hunger of a doe and a fawn roaming outside fences;
the hunger of a mountain lion crossing a freeway;
the hunger of parceled land;
the hunger of a swallow swooping to feed its young;
the hunger of a spawning trout;
the hunger of hatchlings winding to wider waters;
the hunger of crowded roots.
On the boughs of this oak, on this wide slope,
lay down this red, red ribbon.

There will always be hunger like love.
Drink from this red, red vessel.
Drink from cupped hands.
Eat of this blood, this flesh, this heart,
these lips, this tongue, this viscera, this rage,
this placenta, this umbilical cord, this body inside out.

In the grace of these branches bowing in the wind,
in the calm of these redwoods,
there is thirst like a dry creek bed.
A thirsty woman sits by the creek bed.
She asks the sky to send the rain her father felt
as a boy on a houseboat in a deep sound;
the rain on the hard shells of oysters on their soft beds of silt;
oysters with flesh like supple tongues;
oysters with minute pearls on flesh like supple tongues;
the rain on the roof of the houseboat;
the rain on the shoji windows his father built;
the rain on the deck, the rain in the bucket on the deck;
the rain on the pulley, the rain on the rope;
the rain on the water of the deep sound;
the rain on the small boat he rowed from their houseboat to school;
the rain on the spoon his mother clanged on the pot
to guide him home in the fog.

A thirsty woman sits by the dry creek bed.
She softens like the sessile flesh of an oyster;
she hardens like the shell's osseous resistance;
she thinks like a growing pearl, like moonlight,
like the reflection of the moon on a dry creek bed.
There was a time, before her father was born,
pearl meant a concretion of nacre found in oysters,
and *Wai Momi, Pearl Waters* was a lagoon off the coast of Oahu.
Hawaiians fished there. Though oysters were plenty,
they placed no value on pearls. When her father was born,
pearl still meant a concretion of nacre found in oysters;
harbor meant an inlet deep enough to shelter a boat;
Pearl Harbor had been dredged to shelter warships.

By the time he was thirteen, her father was living on a houseboat,
shucking oysters with a dull knife. He held them with care,
as if he loved them—he had learned early how the shells of *kaki*
could cut into his palm like crenellated blades.

He was after small slabs of flesh, small slabs of flesh,
small slabs of flesh, and the sudden gift of a pearl.
Do oysters feel pain?

His buddhist mother and sister were too ashamed to answer.

Small slabs of flesh/*ahimsa*, small slabs of flesh/*ahimsa*,
small slabs of flesh/*ahimsa*…

As the boat rocked:
*dhamma/adhamma, dhamma/adhamma, dhamma/adhamma,
dhamma/adhamma, dhamma/adhamma, dhamma/adhamma*….

His mother and sister would rather count prayer beads than pearls:
*namu-amida-butsu-namu-amida-butsu-namu-amida-butsu-
namu-amida-butsu*….

December 7, 1941
Pearl still meant a concretion of nacre found in oysters;
dhamma/adhamma, dhamma/adhamma, dhamma/adhamma….
Harbor still meant an inlet deep enough to shelter a boat;
dhamma/adhamma, dhamma/adhamma, dhamma/adhamma….
Pearl Harbor, Pearl Harbor, Pearl Harbor, Pearl Harbor….

The family had to leave their houseboat in the sound.
As they looked out from the back of the army truck,
they saw their dog chasing after the them,
[panting] [panting] [panting] [panting]
growing smaller, smaller, smaller, smaller….

Tule is a large, hardstem bulrush:
common tule, hardstem tule,
tule rush, hardstem bulrush, viscid bulrush.
Tule Lake was a camp for no-no boys:
dhamma/adhamma, dhamma/adhamma, dhamma/adhamma....

If there was one in the family, the whole family went—
to stay together.

dhamma/adhamma, dhamma/adhamma, dhamma/adhamma....

A pearl is an oyster's way of protecting itself from foreign substances.
The younger brother of a no-no boy might ask two questions:
Could an oyster sometimes mistake part of its own body
for a foreign substance?
Is there anyone who is not too ashamed to answer this question?

yes-no, no-yes, yes-yes, no-no....
yes-no, no-yes, yes-yes, no-no....

A thirsty woman sits by the dry creek bed.
A hungry woman comes and sits by her.
She asks the earth to send the hunger her father felt as a boy,
the child of a gambler, when dinner was nothing
but rice and soy sauce;
the hunger of a stray cat he took in and fed moistened crackers—
the stray cat he placed on his lap to help him
stay seated while he studied;
his hunger for knowledge; hunger for hunger itself;
his hunger for the loud streets: the cries of hawkers,
the cheers of boys shooting marbles—
his hunger to rise above the streets,
above his father's 天九 *tin¹ gau²* gambling cards:

天 , 地 , 人 , 和 , 梅
tin¹, dei⁶, jan4, wo⁴, mui⁴

heaven, earth, human, harmony, plum flower

九 , 八 , 七 , 六 , 五 , 三
gau², baat³, cat¹, luk⁶, ng⁵, saam¹
nine, eight, seven, six, five, three

above his mother counting the beads of her rosary:
hail mary full of grace, hail mary full of grace,
hail mary full of grace....

At the end of one hill, began another....
At the end of one hill, began another....
Hills like knowledge....
His hunger brought him to this country,
where he studied and studied,
where his wife gave birth to a hungry baby
who would eat nothing but stories and flowers.

Her first word was 花 *faa¹*, flower.
She says to her mother:
teach me the language you speak to your family.
teach me how to count from 1 to 11,
for the 11 daughters in your family.
She asks her mother: where are your lost sisters?
Numbers 3, 4, 10, and 11.
She says, I'll count in the language I speak to you:
三 , 四 , 十 , 十一
saam¹, sei³, sap⁶, sap⁶jat¹
三 , 四 , 十 , 十一
saam¹, sei³, sap⁶, sap⁶jat¹

She asks her mother:
Where are your lost sisters?
What were their favorite flowers?
She says, I would like to show them
how to pluck the petals off a morning glory
and suck the nectar dry.
She asks her mother:

Where are your lost sisters?
Were they given away like pets?
[panting] [panting] [panting] [panting]
growing smaller, smaller, smaller, smaller….

She asks her father:
What was written on the hills you walked?
Where does one hill end and another begin?
Where does one ocean end and another begin?
If you feel with two fingers, how do you know
if you're touching two things, or one continuous surface?
She repeats her little brother's question:
Why does the moon stay in the sky?

She asks the thirsty woman for stories.

The thirsty woman gives her a set of wind chimes made from oyster shells:
yes-no, no-yes, yes-yes, no-no….
yes-no, no-yes, yes-yes, no-no….

The hungry woman builds a raft to cross the dry creek,
adorns it with oyster shells and the names of flowers:

蜘蛛花 *zi¹ zyu¹ faa¹* spider flower
美人蕉 *mei⁵ jan⁴ ziu¹* beautiful maiden banana
薑花 *goeng¹ faa¹* ginger flower
含笑 *ham⁴ siu³* the hidden smile.

When she is finished building the raft,
she sees there is no water in the dry creek bed;
there is no reflection of the moon in the creek bed;
but the moon is shining in the full sky.

莫道水清偏得月，須知水濁亦全天，
mok⁶ dou³ seoi² ceng¹ pin¹ dak¹ jyut⁶
seoi¹ zi¹ seoi² zuk⁶ jik⁶ cyun⁴ tin¹
Don't say the moon shines in clear water only.
In turbid water, there is a clear sky.

請看風定波平後，一顆靈珠依舊圓．
ceng² hon³ fung¹ deng⁶ bo¹ peng⁴ hau⁶
jat¹ fo² ling⁴ zyu¹ ji¹ gau⁶ jyun⁴
Look! When the winds and waters are calm,
the round spirit pearl remains.

She lets go of the raft.
She lets go of the small slabs of flesh/*ahimsa*, small slabs
of flesh/*ahimsa*....
She lets go of the prayer beads:
namu-amida-butsu-namu-amida-butsu-namu-amida-butsu....

She lets go of the questions:
dhamma/adhamma, dhamma/adhamma, dhamma/adhamma....
yes-no, no-yes, yes-yes, no-no....

She lets go of the hunger:
At the end of one hill, began another....
At the end of one hill, began another....

She lets go of the rosary:
hail mary full of grace, hail mary full of grace, hail mary full of grace....

She lets go of the gambling cards:
天，地，人，和，梅
tin¹, dei⁶, jan⁴, wo⁴, mui⁴
heaven, earth, human, harmony, plum flower

She lets go of absence:
三，四，十，十一
3, 4, 10, and 11
saam¹, sei³, sap⁶, sap⁶ jat¹

She lets go of letting go:
[panting] [panting] [panting] [panting]
Growing smaller, smaller, smaller, smaller….

She lets go of the names of flowers:
蜘蛛花 *zi¹ zyu¹ faa¹* spider flower
美人蕉 *mei⁵ jan⁴ ziu¹* beautiful maiden banana
薑花 *goeng¹ faa¹* ginger flower
含笑 *ham⁴ siu³* the hidden smile.

On the boughs of this oak, on this wide slope,
lay down this red, red ribbon.
There is hunger stalking like a coyote.
There will always be hunger like love.
Drink from this red, red vessel.
Eat with bare hands.
Eat from this blood, these vessels, this heart,
these lips, this tongue, this viscera, this rage,
this placenta, this umbilical cord, this body inside out.

On the shared thirst of this dry creek bed,
lay down a river of cloth.
There is the thirst of unhatched eggs.
There will always be absence like thirst.
Drink from this river of cloth.
Drink with cupped hands.
Drink from the sky above.
Drink, and let the sky be.

periodicity

Sunday
 Moonday
    Tiu's day
  Woden's day
      Thor's day

               Freya's day
     Saturn's day

      I am unskilled
      in the
      measure

          of shadows
     and the invocation
         of gods

I'll meet you   let's walk
    somewhere   without
              counting
 on the repeating   our steps
    pattern
   of this

       vast
       fabric

lunar parallax

月亮   *yuè liàng*

jyut⁶ loeng⁶   *a lua*
月 *tsuki*
la lune
    la luna

        I send
         a map
    of the moon
          to Paris

to a lover
 of   he
    one   sends
  night   we
      may
   one back never meet
    again

     how
   I touch
  and lay
    no claim

       how
      I translate
the night   from one
 of the   to
 fullest   the
moon

    next

I bare

myself

with another

by
the lake

my fingers
read

shivers   on
his body

from
the chill
of the night

my touch
on his skin

or the graze

of

an arrow

what
do we use
to write
on the moon

the axe
of a woodcutter   the lance
of São Jorge

the arrow
of Oxóssi   the
arrow of 后羿 *Hòu Yì*
before
we share   嫦娥 *Chángʼé's*
the dark silence   flight
with
stirring ducks
I tone   my
cries
of pleasure

one lover
teaches   me
a   word
saudade
I try
to
translate

longing
like the wet

wick

of a candle
the scuff
of another
lover's stubble
against
my
thigh

                    forgive
                              me
                                   if
                    I miscarry
                         from one language
          to the next
                    some maps
                    are
                         a history   of
               misnomers
               Mare Imbrium
               Mare Frigoris
     Mare Nubium   Mare
               Humorum
          Mare
     Serenitatis

                         Mare
                              Crisium
                                        Oceanus
                         Procellarum

               there are
                                   no seas
                    on the moon

                         if only
               I could   measure
          be
     two places at once   the true
                                             distance
                         from
                              earth
                    to
          moon

Crossings

The desert is dry enough, this parched silence.
The sidewinding snake touches the hot sand
near the head and the tail only.
On this borderland, the wind erases
on sand as in water.
The barbed cactus persists.

At a foundry on a mesa, I left a would-be lover
who spoke eight languages, his eyes like wind inside me.
He stooped under the cave-shaped roof of the foundry,
and handed me a piece of spilled metal
cooled in the sand. I was married then.
I touched him with my eyes only.

No one has drawn maps for black bears
to show the fences they need to cross to reach their mates.
We walk with borrowed bones on sand once under a river.
The earth faults. And waits for our bones to return.
Some risk everything to cross this sand.
If only a snake could grow wings.

sky door

a door
     in the clouds   a door
     opens like lips   in the clouds

opens
         like a book
           in many languages

    how we spin
  in the sky:

    氹氹轉, 菊花園
  tam³ tam³ zyun³, guk¹ faa¹ jyun⁴
  a roundabout,
    a chrysanthemum garden

  a door
in the sky
        longing

    for a lost language:
     Toora loora loora....

        the nearest star
        outshines
          the rest

          daytime
      light obscures light
a door opens
  in a sky
    deceptively bright
       as if to offer
    anyone
      passage

I don't know
what
        the sky looks like
                to a mother
undocumented

the sky
        will not find
    her child   and say:
                la migra
                        has your mother
        but
                she will return

    I don't know
                what the sky
looks like
                from behind barbed wire

                        to a prisoner
                    on death row
                            I don't know
                                if the sky
                        will exonerate
            him

        I've seen the sky
    above a
        lemon
    tree

                            planes
                    taking off
                across the bay

naranja
dulce
limón partido....

a bottle
of white wine
with a lover

an
empty bottle
beside it—

another lover
from the night
before?

as a girl
I heard my mother
sing:

today

while the blossoms
still cling to the vine,

I'll taste your
strawberries   *I'll drink*
your sweet wine
when I

asked
what the lyrics meant

she said
use your imagination

let me
roll   over your
shoulders
again

let me
rest
on my forearms
and look
into your eyes
a door in the sky
could
be a portal
to many places

a door
in the sky
the
promise
of
another country

a door
in the sky
could let
me
through
today
only
where there
is space
at the edge
of the sky
I can watch blue
fade
into white

a student
I never
felt
so alive

walking
to campus
foliage flaming
against the fall sky

I did not
claim
a blue corner
for myself

walking now
with a
new
lover

travelers
in the open night

a creek meanders
through libraries, auditoriums
and lecture halls

shut not your doors
to me
proud libraries

we sit
half hidden
behind a bridge
my fingers   smooth your neck
your mouth searching

                    there
            are stories
                I have not read
                            about
                        travelers
                        in the night

                in the cold of the desert
                a train howls like a beast
                            la bestia
                a train with
                        stories
                untold
there can be
        doors
                where
                there are no walls

                my mother
            birthed me
                on the side of the door
        where the code was inscribed

                    so the guards
                    would
                let me through

                            I

                        leave
                    the door

                            ajar

dictionary of the body

what to call
this tender crook

we
bend
with every footstep

the back
of a claw—
the ankle
or

the eye
of the foot
腳眼 *goek³ ngaan⁵* ?

we
see
as we walk

or shall we
say   *ashikubi*
足首
the head
of the foot?

tobillo
this swelling
tuber

so close
to the ground
quiet corm

                I
            ask   how might   other
                                            words
                            feel
                on my tongue

            it is the fate
of
    the colonized   I
        to speak many
                languages
learn
                    as I walk:
                            cheville—
                        this
                little
                    key   turns
                                        my foot

            I ask   what
                        to
                    call
                                this
                                    swelling
this   腕 *wun²*
    flexure
between   hand
 wrist
                and   la muñeca
                    forearm   this dummy/little
                                        doll

手
　　　the head　　　　　　首
　of　　　　　　　　　*tekubi*
the hand

　　　　　　　　　　　　　as I stand
　　　　　　　　　　　　　on
　　　　my wrist　　　　　my hands
　　　　　　wrestles　with
　　　　my body's
　weight

　　　　it is the fate
　　　　　　　of
the colonized　　　　　　　　I
　　　to　　　　　　　　　　ask
　　　learn　　　　how to use　the
word
　　　　　　poignet
　　　　　　　la lime
　　　est pour mon poignet

　　　　　the file
　　　　is for my wrist

　how the wrist
can　　　　　writhe
under pressure

　　　　　　　　I will betray tomorrow
　　　　je trahirai demain　　*not today*
　　pas aujourd'hui
　　　　　　　demain
　　　　　　　　　tomorrow

today
aujourd'hui   *I have nothing*
        je n'ai rien à dire   to say

                        I will betray tomorrow
            je trahirai
                    demain

            there are many
                        whose words
                    have not
                        survived

resistance
        can be
        a woman's
        smile
for the camera
                                        the smile
                        of a fighter
                                after a fight

            wrists
                untied
                        after
                        and before violation

                成本華 Cheng Ben Hua's
            smile
                for the camera

                brilliant
            as her name: *Hua*
            華

    kuchibiru
                                        chún
            lips   *labios*

a smile
her captors   would   fear
and
remember

idem idem/same same

once
       there was an old man
        who wanted to move
             a mountain
one spoonful   at a time
          at the border
                I would lift
          the fence
             into the sky
if I could
          lend you
this little blue book
        uniform blue
          with my photo in it
          I would

              so a parent
         might hear   their child's
                   voice
my mother
wanted
  to have me
           my mother
      wanted   me
            to have

        this little blue book

     my mother
          wanted
  to have
    this little blue book

so she birthed me
in a land of snow

a land
where the river
lies red
a river
I
don't
remember

a child
of two continents

I was
raised in a city
of many windows
Hong Kong

I would rise from bed
and watch lights
from other windows
as if they were flares
of stories
windows　窗 coeng[1]
wind's eyes

at fourteen
I received an ID
idem idem/same same

to walk
without this card
was to risk arrest

I once raised my voice
in the city of many windows
                shouted on the streets
        the wind's eyes
            stayed open for a glimpse

                        kerítés
    the year barbed wire tore
    walls fell   牆 coeng⁴
Mauer

            guns stuttered
            槍 coeng¹

                    look north
        the rubble of a wall
                no longer   great
        clings   like a scar
    like a   scab
                like a cut
        to reopen

        my ID
now a souvenir—   on the continent
        take a card   of my birth   the little
            any card   blue
                                book is silent

            I write
            to tell

self portrait in vivo

grass
spills
into sunlight

the innermost
tongue
of an orchid

splays in
wild
repose

water
opens to light

what to let pass
if you don't
see
this rainbow
come around
look

from

the angle
of my eyes

if
you
approach
me
like sunlight

I could be
a grain of sand

lucid
as glass

if you
brusque your way
from a sharp angle

you might
find
no
entry   leaves
of the mimosa
fold upon
touch

hold your palm
above
mine

there can be warmth
you are radiant
without touch   I say
I harvest
what I can   show me
the warmth
in you
beyond
my
touch

if
you
split   force
me
begets
open
fissive
force

                    stop
                              before
               you begin

      this kindling
                 body   needs no fuse
                                            to light itself
                     from within

Notes

In "tiens, tiān 天! look, the sky!", *tiens* is "look" in French and *tiān* is "sky" in Chinese.

"locus" references the murder of Vincent Chin in Detroit in 1982.

In "The Quenching," the thirsty woman's story is based on my interview with Judy Shintani. The hungry woman's story is largely autobiographical.

"sky door" is in memory of Francisco X. Alarcón, inspired by a painting he owned. *La migra* refers to immigration authorities. *La bestia*, the beast, is a network of freight trains undocumented migrants take from Mexico into the US.

"dictionary of the body" draws from the stories of two women in World War II: the French resistance fighter Marianne Cohn's poem *"Je trahirai demain"* and a photo of the Chinese resistance fighter Cheng Ben Hua 成本華.

"self portrait in vivo" was inspired by visits to the nanophotonics laboratory of The Dionne Group at Stanford University.

$\mathbf{B}$onnie Wai-Lee Kwong is a poet, multidisciplinary artist, engineer, and mother of two children. Her work in poetry and fiction has garnered six Pushcart nominations, and appeared in journals such as *The California Quarterly, The Columbia Review, Crab Orchard Review, The Pedestal, Nimrod,* and *Taos Journal of International Poetry and Art.* Her first book of poetry, *ravel,* was a finalist for prizes by White Pine Press and New Rivers Press. *Liriope,* her first play, was staged at Stanford University's Jasper Ridge Biological Preserve. Her second play, *There's No Stopping to My Thoughts,* was staged at the Oakland Asian Cultural Center with a grant from the California Arts Council (CAC).

www.ingramcontent.com/pod-product-compliance
Lightning Source LLC
Chambersburg PA
CBHW021202090426
42740CB00008B/1194